Presented to:

From:

Date:

Prayer & Meditation

Meditation

A Practical Guide to the Life Promised in Step 11

Cover photograph courtesy of Alima Blackwell
Cover design by Gail Sheehan

Tom R.
Practically Spiritual Books
4585 Shoshone St., Ste. 104
Denver, CO 80211

www.PracticallySpiritualBooks.com

First printing June 2013

ISBN 978-1-61704-186-0

For worldwide distribution. Printed in U.S.A.

FOREWORD

In 2009, I met Tom R. and became interested in what he told me of his Step 11 practice. I became one of the first two members to join him at his house where we would take 45 minutes to an hour and practice Step 11 as it is explained in this book. At the time, I had 5 years of sobriety—more like so-dry-iety! and was not a happy camper! When I began experiencing the ideas presented in this book by practicing them on a daily basis, I emailed Tom R. and wrote "It's TRUE, the spiritual life is NOT a theory!!!!" I went from being a dry, hopelessly depressed AA member with 5 years of sobriety—who was contemplating suicide—to quickly finding my purpose and passion for life through a relationship with what I discovered is a loving and amazing God. Our prayer and meditation group met morning after morning, practicing this Step 11 work and receiving its promises. We all "kept coming back" because we learned to truly have contact and relationship with this God the Big Book speaks of so frequently. As Step 11 in the Big Book promises, we were constantly surprised. God transformed our hearts as we sat together each morning to seek knowledge of his will for us and the power to carry it out. We each found that while regular AA meetings were good, they were simply not enough. We each hungered for something more, and we found what we hungered for during our times together each morning, with God.

Tom R's book is a collection of "how to" suggestions from AA's literature on Step 11, as well as different members' personal experiences. It is compiled in a user-friendly way that will teach you how you can put together a prayer and meditation practice the way AA's founders did.

The methods Tom R. teaches are tried and true. I urge you to take the techniques discussed in this book and make them your own and make them the centerpiece of your 12-step work. Learning how to have a relationship with God is the greatest gift I have received in my life and it took my own experience with the 12-step work to a deeper level then I could have imagined. Doing the daily exercises in this book is how I got it.

Read on and try this!

God bless.

Jessi R.

TABLE OF CONTENTS

Page

TABLE OF CONTENTS
(continued)

Page

ENDORSEMENTS FOR STEP 11 RETREATS

What a wonderful weekend . . . enlightening, and on-going. Thank you for this gift. See you at morning P&M! *Lisa R., Seattle*

I'm still basking in the wonderful glow of the great energy, relaxation, communication and camaraderie. Thank you everyone for making me feel so welcome. The P&M tribe – you all did a fantastic job preparing the agenda and materials to share with us. It was so obviously a labor of love. I'm looking forward to trying again to get something going here in Dallas. *Michael H.*, Dallas

Great content, place, people, energy, and experience. *Jill F., Seattle*

Wonderful to soak in the Spirit with you all. Wonderful teaching. Great facilitation. Thanks! *Dave W., Rainier Beach, WA*

Thank you again for an entirely wonderful weekend. My heart was touched, and hopefully a few walls came down. . . . I have been buzzing since I left. . . . Many blessings to the P&M tribe! *Duffy H., Olympia*

Blessings to you! Brent and I just wanted to send our heartfelt thanks for your work and your generosity of spirit in planning and leading the Step 11 Retreat this weekend. We both feel such a deep peace and joy! We're looking forward to doing daily prayer together, and attending another retreat this fall. All the best, *Brent and Angela S., Seattle*

Thank you for an outstanding weekend of P&M. Your wisdom and insight have helped Step 11 take on a new meaning. All of the exercises practiced this weekend will be incorporated into my daily meditation. Love you all a bunch! *Cherrise G., Seattle*

The retreat put me solidly on track, and I am so grateful! I have meditated for long periods in the past, but have been disconnected for some time. I love this method of meditation as it's much shorter than what I was doing, and I find it just as effective. It's a simple and easy practice. My days and sleep have been calm and peaceful. I have meditated every day but one – and that has been my only "not-wonderful" day. I keep thinking of the phrase "daily reprieve" that my first sponsor reminded me of when I - frequently - lost my connection with God. It's still true! *Grace, Seattle*

I've been sober 18 years, and this is the first time I've ever meditated consistently. Sleeping better, smiling and laughing more, have less worries, and things seem to be unfolding in such synchronistic ways. I'll keep coming back. *Alice C., Bothell, WA*

ACKNOWLEDGMENTS

Mark S., my sponsor. The first thing you did for me, beginning the first day we met, was an introduction to the invisible: "God, meet Tom; Tom, meet God." Each week, before we would open the book, *Alcoholics Anonymous*, and read, you took me through five minutes of directed meditation. It turned out to be the same way Joe McIntyre had shown me 30 years before. Thank you for this new way of living that you opened up to me, and for your ongoing grace in my life. It was worth waiting for. **Mark** found **me**, consistent with the direction in the Big Book, *Alcoholics Anonymous* "*. . . when we were approached by someone in whom the problem had been solved."* This is the AA way. The recovered alcoholic or addict approaches the sick one. You did that, and continue to do so, day after day. You presented the clearest path out, using only the directions found in the Big Book, from the title page to page 164.

Jessi R. and Glenn T. You were the first to believe in what was possible by following these directions, and you came every morning. We were truly *The Three Amigos!* This book would never have been written without you.

John M. ("John the Cop"), a member of my home group, Abigail's Ghost, in Seattle, Washington. John, you moved me further down the path of daily morning devotion when you shared what you did every morning: four familiar prayers, reading pages 86-88 from the Big Book, *Alcoholics Anonymous*, and writing.

Wally P., archivist for Dr. Bob, shared a lost treasure, the *"How to Listen to God"* exercise that Dr. Bob brought into AA from the Oxford Group.

Gail Sheehan and Linda Coleman, Ph.D., for your editing and proofreading expertise. You made it purdy! Any final mistakes, errors, or omissions are mine.

Special Thanks to the following friends who helped get this book to the printer with last minute help (in the 11th hour—get it?): Roy H. (Seattle), Linda C. (Olympia), Mary L. (Olympia) Danelle A. (Denver), Dave A. (Seattle), Glenn T., Christin Crowley (Baltimore), Jeff N, Duffy N. (Olympia), and Donna E. (Denver).

I probably have forgotten other important people. Please forgive me, and make an appointment at your earliest convenience to make your amends to me for your resentment. (That's my sponsor's idea of humor).

DEDICATION

"Lack of Power, that was our dilemma." Ah, yes. That's been the "backstory" for so much of my life. But, *"There is One who has ALL power, may you find Him now!"*

God. I would like to dedicate this small volume to the One who knows me best and loves me most. You have been there, *"through many dangers, trials and snares."* You have never given up on me (despite my best efforts to push you away), and you have even factored my stupidity into your plan for my life. I hope you are pleased with this small volume, and that You grace the words here to help others as they've helped me. Today, I live for an audience of One.

Joe McIntyre, author, teacher, friend. Joe, you are someone I've considered closer than a brother for the last 40 years. You opened this way of life to me in February, 1973, and you continue to live it before me, as the best example I've ever seen. You are the embodiment of an AA passage, *"The spiritual life is not a theory; we have to live it."*[1] I came to believe because **you** first believed, and carried that message to me. You found a way to believe in me, and when I would falter, you would pick me back up and fill me with hope. I'll never be able to thank you enough.

---

[1] *Alcoholics Anonymous,* p. 83.

Family. I would like to express my gratitude to my dad, Harry, who went before me (sober in 1961) and my brothers: Rick, Dave, and Mike. You stood by me through my first attempts at sobriety and often extended shelter, food, encouragement, and comfort—all one could ever expect of the very best brothers. Thank you.

Robert McN. My first sponsor (Houston, TX). You never gave up on me, and you were the first one in AA to give me hope. Thank you. I'm so happy we have reconnected after 25 years.

My AA Teachers. Finally, I dedicate this volume my teachers: The prayer and meditation communities in Seattle, Olympia, and Kent, Washington and Denver, Colorado. You enabled me to see the beauty and the power of doing this together by fulfilling the directions on page 87: *"If circumstances warrant, we ask our wives or friends to join us in morning meditation."* It's true. It really does make a difference.

PREFACE

"Mistaken identity is the source of all spiritual sickness."

So, the question is this: **Why are *you* here**?

That's the first question I ask at the start of any workshop or retreat.

I'm not asking why you are here, in this book, but **here** on this planet, a part of this universe? Do you *have* a purpose? Is there some sort of grand plan, some divine purpose, or were you just an accident?

Page 68 of the Big Book gives us an answer: "*We are in the world to play the role He assigns.*" So. Why are **you** here? What is **your** role that God has assigned?

You may reply when faced with this question, "*Heaven only knows*!!"

Our question may be, at that point, how do we *discover* that role? How do we find out who we really are, and why we are here? To borrow a line from *We Agnostics*, "*Well, that is exactly what this book is about.*[2]"

---

[2] *Alcoholics Anonymous*, p. 45.

The Search for Meaning

Identity is essential to our understanding of the spiritual life. The question, *"Who am I?"* often begins with an attempt to understand how we got to where we are. Who has been telling me who I am? Who have I been listening to for clues, for answers? My Dad? My Mom? Teachers? Lawyers? Judges? Bosses? Girl/boyfriend? Though often well-intentioned, it is impossible for any human being to provide the answers we seek. One fellow seems to have found clarity on his own identity when he had a "God encounter." On page 158 of the Big Book, *Alcoholics Anonymous,* we are told about this man, *". . . he found God; and in finding God, he found himself."*[3]

That is the journey we must be on if we are to discover who we are, and why we are here. If you are not certain why you are here or what your purpose is, let me assure you: you have a place and a purpose in God's plan. Discovering your place and your purpose in this world *is* the Great Adventure!

Perhaps you are new in recovery, new to the journey, or are newly discovering this path after many years of sobriety. Maybe you're a doubter or a skeptic. It's possible that no matter how long you have been sober or have been struggling to get sober, the idea and reality of faith may have escaped you. This might be a good time to start fresh. The Set Aside Prayer is a good place to begin.

---

[3] *Ibid.*, p. 158.

God; please enable me to set aside everything I think I know about myself, other people, these Steps, and especially You, so that I can have an open mind and a new experience with myself, other people, these Steps, and especially You!

First Thoughts

If you don't know where you're going, any road will take you there. Anonymous

May I ask you some questions for your initial consideration?

1. Raise your (inner) hand if you feel you spend **too much** time each day in prayer and meditation;

2. Raise your (inner) hand if you feel you spend **just about the right** time each day in prayer and meditation;

3. Finally, raise your (inner) hand if you feel you **could spend more time**, be more consistent, or be more effective in prayer and meditation than you are.

If you answered "yes" to questions #1 and #3, this book will give you new direction and hope.

If you're already doing it well, congratulations! Hopefully you will find additional tools that are useful to you or someone you know.

Our Goals

1. **Improved conscious contact with God**. What would that look like for you? Hearing God better, knowing God's will with more certainty?

2. **Wholeness**. Sobriety (spiritual), sanity (mental), and good health (physical). Have you considered that God wants you not only sober, but **whole**?

> *Is sobriety all that we are to expect of a spiritual awakening? No, sobriety is <u>only a bare beginning</u>; it is only the **first gift** of the **first awakening**. If more gifts are to be received, our awakening has to go on. As it does go on, we find that bit by bit we can discard the old life—the one that did not work—for a new life that can and does work under any conditions whatever.*[4] (emphasis mine)

Why does this quote, from co-founder, Bill W. say "*sobriety is only a bare beginning*?" Strictly speaking, most of us think of sobriety as freedom from alcohol, drugs, overeating, or whatever else ails us. Discarding the old life spoken of here is not simply discarding a substance, but being freed from an entire a way of living that "does not work." Surely, I must be free *from* the addiction, but *into* what life?

---

[4] *Grapevine*, 1957.

3. Usefulness to God and Our Fellows.

> *Our main purpose is to fit ourselves to be maximum usefulness to God* ***and the people about us***.[5] (emphasis mine)

As I come into true intimacy ("*in-to-me-see*") with my Creator and others, I discover the design God had for me from the beginning. As I find that, I come to know true peace and contentment—no matter what my outward circumstances are. I'll know my identity, destiny and purpose.

[Please note: this book is intended to be a textbook. So please write in it, scribble on it, study it, question it. Make use of the space provided at the end of certain chapters to make notes.]

---

[5] *Alcoholics Anonymous*, p. 77

Cathy's Story

On July 5, 1984, I was in a head-on automobile accident with a drunk driver, at 110 mph (combined impact). I was 30 years old, and this was before my drinking had become a problem. I was taken to the hospital with a 10% chance of living, a severe concussion and a serious brain injury.

Several days later, I came out of my coma and a doctor explained to me that I was so brain injured that I would never be able to work again. He told me that I would be on Social Security disability for the rest of my life, and that I would need 24-hour nursing care, probably for the rest of my life as well. He also told me that there was nothing else that could be done for me, and that in the history of the hospital, the staff had never seen anyone hurt this badly and survive. They had no treatment recommendations available to help me with my recovery. Much later, I was released from the hospital with a 50% chance of living.

I went back to my apartment to recover and rehabilitate under a nurse's care. During that time, I was in a lot of pain. One day, some neighbors invited me over to their home and offered me a drink, saying "This will help you feel less pain." I didn't know that medical studies had determined that while someone is recovering from a brain injury, they cannot tolerate alcohol. I had a very scary reaction to that glass of wine and my nurse/caregiver got very angry. She told me that I must not, under any circumstances, consume alcohol. However, that glass of wine started a craving for alcohol and I found myself wanting more.

At that time, I did not know that alcoholism ran in my family, so I didn't realize I was in jeopardy of triggering this disease. I just thought anyone suffering the level of pain that I was should be allowed a glass of wine, and I managed to find ways to get more alcohol. I eventually drank myself back into a coma. This was before I learned that for me, "to drink is to die." Given the circumstances, there was no nursing service that wanted to take responsibility for me, and I was relocated from Florida to Washington State, to live with my parents, who would have to be my caregivers.

Unbelievably, that accident turned out to be a source of incredible blessings for me, for my family and for many others. Although I didn't have a Twelve-Step program at that time, I did follow the instructions contained in the book, Alcoholics Anonymous. I turned my will and my life over to the care of God. Over the next few years I learned many lessons, such as:

- Miracles do happen
- God loves me and wants the best for me
- With God, anyone can walk through anything

- God answers prayers more abundantly and generously than anyone can dream
- Good things can come out of bad circumstances, if you turn them over to God

I finally made my way to the rooms of Alcoholics Anonymous and was introduced to the Program that would help me create a life that was worth living. Over the next few years, the symptoms of my brain injury faded, and I managed to become employable – to the surprise of all of the doctors who had been involved in my case. I was going to meetings and working the Steps with my AA sponsor. My life improved quite a bit and I believe it was because I was doing the work of the AA Program to the best of my ability.

In November of 2010, a friend invited me to a Prayer & Meditation retreat in Seabeck, Washington. At that time, I had been sober over 10 years. During my recovery from the brain injury, I had learned to accept gifts and direction from God when they appeared in front of me, so I accepted this invitation, although I didn't really expect to get much out of it. Was I ever wrong!

That weekend changed my life.

I had been trying to learn how to meditate since the 1970s, but without success. I tried several different types of meditation: Transcendental, Buddhist, New-Age, etc. All of those disciplines started with the instruction to quiet your mind, which I had never been able to do. Tom R. presented an approach to meditation that I could understand and put into practice. His approach didn't expect me to be able to create a blank mind. All I had to do during meditation was focus on the meaning of just one word or phrase at a time, such as "GOD ... LOVES ... ME." I could do that.

Before the weekend ended, we were told to find a P&M (prayer and meditation) "buddy," and commit to doing 90 meditation sessions in 90 days with that person. The assignment was to take time to pray and meditate, then to phone, text, or email the messages we received during the session to our P&M buddy, every day for 90 days. I got a buddy and we did this daily.

Prior to my doing P&M every day, I was really struggling with the frustrations of not having a good memory, as a result of the accident. Because I forgot so many things, I began making careful, copious notes about everything! Sometimes I can't even remember where I parked my car! Managing time was also difficult for me. Many things that other people handle easily were simply too hard to accomplish.

The daily stress I was living with had turned me into what my husband called "an angry woman." I was snapping at the least provocation and yelling to release tension. The nickname my friends gave me was "Crazy Cathy" because I was so emotional. I over-reacted and my life often became chaotic.

Thankfully, my friends somehow accepted my turbulent nature and merely considered me "interesting" and "fun to watch."

Even my family members became worn out from the emotional storms that constantly ran through my life. They were also the first to notice the difference in me after I began a consistent practice of P&M. My husband began to comment on how much calmer I was and how much more he enjoyed my company. My son was amazed that I could just sit still and watch the birds in my yard for long periods of time. Prior to my new, daily P&M practice, I felt compelled to focus constantly on trying to do more than what others expected -- to prove I was capable of being a good wife and mother. When I heard their comments I realized how much easier and more manageable my life had become.

I was so excited by the success of the P&M process and what I was getting out of it that I continued journaling my daily sessions, even after I didn't have a "buddy" waiting for my text messages. Several months later, my P&M buddy texted me that she had gotten out of the habit of doing daily P&M sessions, and we agreed to do another 90-in-90.

After a while, my friends and acquaintances also started noticing a difference in me. They commented on my calmness and happiness. I told people about what P&M was doing for me, and several people became quite interested. I asked if they also wanted to receive my text messages.

Several did, so I created a meditation group on my cell phone. I wanted to show people that if "Crazy Cathy" could manage to pray and meditate every day and get positive results, anyone could!

After people started getting my daily texts, interest in P&M grew in my area. I asked Tom R. if he would to lead a P&M session in my home. He agreed and led two separate, four-hour P&M sessions for people who wanted to learn about what I had discovered. About 15-25 people attended each session. As a result, other people expressed a desire to receive my P&M messages daily.

Today, I text my daily meditations to 20 people, and some of them text their meditations back to the group. Now, it has become a P&M community of support. We pray for each other, and help each other get through difficult times.

There are days when I get amazing "*Ah ha*!" messages. Other days I just get good ideas about how to live a better life. Overall, the process has been very enlightening, inspiring, calming, and comforting. After I text a meditation, I frequently get a response from someone saying something like "*Thank you for that message*" or "*Oh my God, that is exactly what I needed to hear today*!" This type of feedback has encouraged me to continue with the practice, even on my busiest days. Sometimes the messages I get don't seem to apply to me, but I later hear that it really helped someone else. Perhaps God is using me as a channel to reach others on those days.

I am delighted by the changes that I am experiencing on a consistent basis because of the practice of P&M. For instance, I had a difficult time letting go of an old resentment dating back several years, despite continuous efforts to "Let Go, Let God." I registered mentally that the answer was acceptance, but I couldn't get that message to travel the distance between my brain and my heart. For some reason, I still couldn't release what was bothering me. Recently, I realized that somehow, over the time I have been meditating on a daily basis, total acceptance of the situation has occurred. In meditation one morning a thought about the situation came to mind, and I noticed that thinking about it didn't upset me. I heard myself say "*Wow, this is how acceptance feels*!" Through practicing P&M on a daily basis, acceptance has become a reality for me, not just a concept.

I am having similar experiences with the concepts of peace and serenity. I am enjoying the ability to sit quietly "in my own skin" and be comfortable. It is wonderful to realize that I can still be so teachable. I try to stay open to receiving blessings, messages, direction, and guidance from God. Amazingly, my life continues to get better!

The consistent practice of Prayer & Meditation has freed me of old burdens and baggage. It has helped me learn how to live more comfortably and peacefully. Today, I don't get as agitated and upset by the memory problems I experience. Thus, the problems that occur don't escalate like they used to do. My life and my medical condition are much improved as a result of P&M. Now, I am more likely to respond to my problems with a degree of calm acceptance and perspective, rather than my previous reactions of extreme frustration, anger, and resentment, followed by an outbreak of rampant emotions. Meditation has really improved my life and it's much less expensive than therapy!

Improving my connection with God is the most exciting adventure I have ever experienced! I have found that getting messages through meditation is like using a muscle: the more I exercise it the stronger it gets. Now I know that God is my personal trainer! My messages today are even more meaningful than those I received during the first couple of months I was practicing meditation.

I continue to make time to meditate every morning, and I also find time to do it throughout the day to reduce stress and increase my awareness and acceptance of what life holds for me. I feel more blessed today, probably because I am more aware of the blessings that were always there.

Daily, I try to turn my will and my life over to God, continually asking for His will for my life. It's not very surprising that my life has gotten a lot better during the time I've been working with this process. God wants me to have the best and to be the best I can be. He wants more for me than I can imagine. As long as I cooperate with God, and His plan for my life, my life is good and it keeps getting better!

A Totally Different Person

People who have known me for years have commented that the change they have seen in me over the last three years (since I started meditating) is remarkable. My sponsor recently said, "*When you speak at meetings, I wish the newcomers could have heard how you spoke 2 or 3 years ago, so they could have perspective to compare with who you are today. You've become a totally different person. You have so much more of the right stuff to offer now.*" My program has a whole new dimension since I've become so consistent regarding working Step 11 and trying daily to improve my conscious contact with God.

Recently, I met with someone whom I had sponsored years ago. She had previously asked to be on my meditation texting list and has been reading my messages for several months. After not seeing each other in person for years, we met for coffee to catch up. We talked for a while and then she looked at me and blurted out, "*Cathy, I want what you have*!" She was amazed at the change in me. She wants me to sponsor her again and to teach her how to meditate. I have more to offer others today, because I am always asking God to fill me and to use me as a tool to do His will. Tom R. has a saying, "*First you fill, then you spill*" (onto others).

I believe that God wants to fill all of our lives with goodness and love. He also wants us to achieve spiritual growth so that we can be closer to Him. P&M opens the channel to allow that process to occur more fully. Today, my relationship with God is deeper, richer, and fuller than I could have dreamed possible. My life is better and more enjoyable and I believe I am a better and more enjoyable person to be around. I believe this is happening because on a daily basis I set "me" aside, and I invite God in. As the God in me grows, my life and the relationships I value all improve.

I hope everyone who reads this makes a commitment to start practicing P&M daily! Meditation will help you get more in touch with God and be more aware of God in others. You can significantly improve your life and the lives of those around you when you spend time in prayer and meditation. I KNOW you will be rewarded for the time you spend improving your conscious contact with God. I have seen it work for a lot of people.

Of all the things I have learned so far, I know I am much less stressed when I leave the big picture to God and just try to do my part. I ask God each morning for His will for my life.

I am so grateful for my recoveries and for my connection to my Higher Power! Learning to meditate has made a HUGE difference in my life!

Fulfill God's plan for your life: Become the best you can be. Experience acceptance, peace, serenity, and gratitude. Improve your connection with your

Higher Power. Enjoy life more fully. Share the greatness with others.

Embrace the blessings!

Cathy C.

Why Does Prayer and Meditation Matter?

Almost any experienced AA will tell how his affairs have taken remarkable and unexpected turns for the better as he tried to improve his conscious contact with God.[6]

So, why find out about prayer and meditation? Why begin (or restart) this adventure? There are at least four reasons for the recovering person.

First, life has little meaning until we discover who we are and what we are here for. A life without meaning is hardly worth living.

Life + meaning—now *there's* a life!

Second, it matters because we are instructed to do it. Step 11 (pages 85-88) reveals that this is the only Step where clear, specific, instructions are given for each morning and evening; how we can practice these timeless disciplines each and every day. In other words, I only have to work this Step on the mornings I plan "on awakening" and the nights I intend to go to sleep!

---

[6] Twelve Steps and Twelve Traditions, p. 105.

Third, the practice of serious, consistent prayer and meditation was key to AA's early success with drunks (a 93% success ratio in Akron/Cleveland):[7]

> *Morning quiet time continued to be an important part of the recovery program in early 1938-39 as did the spiritual reading from which the early members derived a good deal of their inspiration.*[8]

and

> *Duke [early Toledo AA member] remembered taking a poll of "slippers" in the early 1940s and finding that they had all stopped having their morning quiet time.*[9]
>
> *The AA members of the time (1938) did not consider meetings necessary to maintain sobriety. They were simply "desirable." Morning devotion and 'quiet time,' however, were musts.*[10]

And finally, from Bill Wilson's closing speech at the 1955 AA International Convention in St. Louis,

---

[7] They kept track!

[8] *Dr. Bob and the Good Oldtimers*, New York, NY: AA World Services, Inc., 1980, pp. 150-55.

[9] *Dr. Bob and the Good Oldtimers*, New York, NY: AA World Services, Inc., 1980, pp. 150-55.

[10] Quoting Frank D. Amos, one of AA's first nonalcoholic trustees; *Dr. Bob and the Good Oldtimers*, New York, NY: AA World Services, Inc., 1980, p. 136.

summing up the importance of seeking, finding, and doing God's will:

> *In AA we have two dictators, and we profit and grow through both. One is John Barleycorn, who is never very far from the elbow of each of us. The other is the Father of Lights, who presides over all men. God is saying to us, "Learn my will and do it." And John Barleycorn is saying to each of us, "You had better do God's will—or I will kill you!"*[11] *(*emphasis mine*)*

Thus, we discover our practical need for developing a relationship with the One who has all power, if we are to live comfortably and usefully in this new life. The book, *Twelve Steps and Twelve Traditions*, tells us prayer and meditation are our principal means of gaining, maintaining, and expanding this conscious contact with God.

> *. . . If you saw your life as a great battle and you knew you needed time with God for your very survival, you would do it. Maybe not perfectly—nobody ever does, and that's not the point anyway—but you would have a reason to seek him. We give a half-hearted attempt at the spiritual disciplines when the only reason we have is that we "ought" to.*

---

[11] Bill Wilson, closing address at St. Louis, 1955 (*AA Comes of Age*, p. 225).

But we'll find a way to make it work when we are convinced we're history if we don't.[12]

NOTES:

____

____

____

____

____

____

____

____

[12] John Eldredge, *Wild at Heart*.

Introduction

In the chapter, We Agnostics, we read the **main** purpose of the book, *Alcoholics Anonymous*:

> *Its main object is to enable you to find a Power greater than yourself which will solve your problem.*[13]

The Problem? Separation from God.

We are told the Twelve Steps enable us to face the things in us that have created this separation and to have them removed. One purpose of the Steps, then, is to remove the things that block us from God and ignite conscious contact.

Once we have found that the Power exists and is available, we learn to access it, and continue accessing it so that this Power might continue to "*solve our problems*." Several times the Big Book indicates that this experience is designed to do more than enable us to recover from alcohol or drug addiction. It's only the beginning!

> *Is sobriety all that we are to expect of a spiritual awakening? No, sobriety is only a bare beginning; it is only the first gift of the first awakening. If more gifts are to be*

[13] *Alcoholics Anonymous*, p. 45.

received, our awakening has to go on. As it does go on, we find that bit by bit we can discard the old life—the one that did not work—for a new life that can and does work under any conditions whatever.[14]

The Big Book says that this Power will "*solve my problems,*" ***plural***.[15] To do that, we must take a thorough Step 1: surrender, surrender, surrender. Like Bill says about his friend, Ebby T., "*. . . he admitted complete defeat.*[16]" Whenever we are restless, irritable, or discontented, we may discover that there is often something we have not yet surrendered. As a consequence, we may feel a disconnection from God.

We approach the practice of prayer and meditation as the primary means for accessing more and more power to solve more and more problems, as well as the means to discover God's will for our lives, and the power to carry it out.

I've done my best to make this journey with you positive, simple, and fun; an *experience*. Adding more knowledge without the opportunity to

---

[14] *Grapevine*, December 1957

[15] Reference to the steps as a means of solving all my problems occurs at least 11 times.

[16] *Alcoholics Anonymous*, p. 11.

internalize these truths does little good,[17] so we'll present the opportunity to do both learn and practice.

Consider the following terms and their definitions. This is what we will be doing.

Cognitive: Of or pertaining to the **mental** processes of perception, memory, judgment, and reasoning, as contrasted with **emotional** and **volitional** processes.

Experiential: A particular instance of personally encountering or undergoing something. Relating to or derived from *experience*—the *doing* of an idea. "*The criterion which we use to test the genuineness of apparent statements of fact.*"[18] Knowledge or practical wisdom gained from what one has encountered or undergone. "*Knowing in your knower.*"

In philosophy the word experiential means the totality of the cognitions given by perception; all that is perceived, understood, and remembered. It is knowledge, fulfilled.

Sound caution: [resistance] We must not fear failure or temporary setbacks as we learn.

---

[17] Imagine saying I know how to ride a bike, because I read a book on bike riding, but never got on one! So, we will do both cognitive and experiential footwork.

[18] Ayer.

If we are not free to fail, as we step into places we've never been and do things we've never done, we'll not take the risks necessary into the unknown, to move us from where we are, to where we are to go. Anonymous

We're human. We often fumble forward.

Someone once advised me that when expertise is needed, find someone who has failed and risen again, rather than someone who (says) they've not known failure (liar!). It's easy to give advice when your success has cost you little.

- **Hindrances/ Obstacles.**
  - **Prejudices**. The Big Book warns us "*Do not let any prejudice you may have against spiritual terms deter you from honestly asking yourself what they mean to you.*"[19]
  - **Fear of making mistakes**. Mistakes are not obstacles but opportunities; portals to new discoveries.
  - **Lack of forgiveness**. I've learned some valuable lessons along the way about the power and necessity of forgiveness. I've learned them, of course, the hard way:

---

[19] *Alcoholics Anonymous,* p. 47.

- <u>Forgiveness is a decision, not an emotion</u>. That means I can *choose* to forgive. The Big Book characterizes this as "*. . . the proper use of the will*." [20]

- <u>Forgiveness is enlightened self-interest</u>. A certain man was counseling a woman for months who had been poorly treated for most of her marriage by her husband. He cheated, drank up their money, and beat her. Finally, they divorced. This counselor listened to her for weeks, and eventually advised her, "*You know, at some point you have to forgive him*." "*Forgive him?*" she queried. "*He ruined 20 years of my life?!!*" Then, with the wisdom he was known for, the counselor responded, "*Do you want him to ruin the next 20*"? (Forgiveness does <u>not</u> mean you return to the situation or say it's okay, of course.)

- <u>Forgiveness *extended* opens the door to forgiveness received</u>. According to a survey published in *The Grapevine*, 73% of AA still uses *The Lord's Prayer* as their primary prayer. In that prayer, we pray "forgive us our trespasses **AS** we forgive those who trespass against us." No forgiveness for others, no forgiveness for me. No forgiveness, no freedom. The

---

[20] Alcoholics Anonymous, p. 85

resentment I hold against someone may be the very thing that's blocking me from conscious contact with God. It can be removed.

Why not take a moment right now, close your eyes, and ask God for the names of people against whom you hold any resentment, anger, bitterness, or hatred. Any debt which you have refused to cancel. As you "hear" the names, write them down.

Next, put your hand over the names and pray a forgiveness prayer such as the following:

God, I don't want anything or anyone, past or present, to keep me from a new experience with You. Therefore, I am choosing to forgive all of the persons (or institutions) on this list, whether I feel like it or not. I know I must forgive if I am to be forgiven. I cancel their debt right now, at ____________ a.m./p.m. Amen.

Baggage: Lay Your Burden Down

Backpacks are useful. I carried one to work each day. In it are the things I need for the hours at work: papers, calendar, books for lunchtime reading. I also sometimes carry things I had in my backpack yesterday (like old food), but forgot to unload when I got home the night before. I call this "yesterday's baggage." Like my illustration, we often carry things around from day to day, without emptying the backpack out. Emotionally, we carry hurts, resentments, fears, worries, etc., for days, without resolving them. So, our emotional and spiritual backpack gets heavier and heavier. It can happen so slowly, so gradually, so subtly, that I often don't notice until, literally, my shoulders ache and my back is sore.

So, will you take a moment right now, and close your eyes with me? Next, imagine all the "cares" you have in your own backpack—concerns about money, job, relationships, children, neighbors, coworkers, friends, siblings, sponsor, sponsee(s). Ugh. I can feel the weight even as I type this!

Now, slip one thumb through one shoulder strap, and gently slide it off. Next, do the same to the other shoulder strap. Then, lower it slowly to the ground. (Careful, now! You may want to pick some of that back up!)

There.

Doesn't that feel better?

Now, we're ready.

Let's begin.

Chapter 1

WHAT IT'S NOT

Step 11: *"Sought through prayer and meditation to improve our conscious contact with God as we understood Him, praying only for knowledge of His will for us and the power to carry that out."*

This small volume suggests a general approach for practicing Step 11. It is useful for all faiths. It is not a particular religious approach; not specifically Hindu, Buddhist, Christian, Moslem, or Jewish. Why? Let's look at a few texts from the book, *Alcoholics Anonymous*.

- *We have no desire to convince anyone that there is only one way by which [this] faith can be acquired. If what we have learned and felt and seen means anything at all, it means that all of us, whatever our race, creed, or color are the children of a living Creator with whom we may upon simple and understandable terms as soon as we are willing and honest enough to try. (p. 28).*

- *We represent no particular faith or denomination. We are dealing only with general principles. . . . (pp. 93-94).*

- *To us, the Realm of Spirit is broad, roomy, all inclusive; never exclusive or forbidding to those who earnestly seek. (p. 46).*

- *Let us make haste to reassure you. We found that as soon as we were able to lay aside prejudice and express even a willingness to believe in a Power greater than ourselves we commenced to get results, even though it was impossible for any of us to fully define or comprehend that Power, which is God. (p. 46).*

NOTES:

Chapter 2

What It Is

Step 11: *"Sought through prayer and meditation to improve our conscious contact with God as we understood Him, praying only for knowledge of His will for us and the power to carry that out."*

"Yes! Live! Life's a banquet and most poor suckers are starving to death!" Auntie Mame, 1958

Let's go for a ride!!

Let's pret[illegible]re on a roadtrip. T[illegible]cle is our transportat[illegible] It's our God-seekin[illegible]t! We've checked the tires, we've filled up the tank. The model? The Prayer & Meditation SUV! Keep your eyes open—it's a big road ahead!

Is sobriety all we are to expect of a spiritual awakening? No, sobriety is only a bare

> *beginning; it is only the first gift of the first awakening. If more gifts are to be received, our awakening has to go on. As it does go on, we find that bit by bit we can discard the old life—the one that did not work—for a new life that can and does work under any conditions whatever.*[21]

Let's look at some of the vocabulary used in Step 11 of the Big Book, *Alcoholics Anonymous*.

- **Seek/Sought**.

We **see** God when we **seek** God. This Step is about the seeking, and the finding. When I was just a kid, I was really good at finding objects that were lost. If someone in our family lost something, they came to me to find it. Like a young Inspector Clouseau, I would set about my assignment *until* I found the missing prize.

Remarkably, some say the goal for us is the *seeking*, not in the finding. That doesn't match with what this Step tells us. How long do you think my family would have continued to ask me to find lost treasures if I came back to them and said, "No, I didn't find it, but I had a wonderful time looking!" **Seeking** without **finding** leads only to frustration. We seek **in order** to find. How long would you play "Hide and Seek" if you never found what you were looking for?

---

[21] *Grapevine*, December 1957.

- **through (via) Prayer**.

Our means of "*finding*" comes through prayer. (See Chapter 6)

- **and [through] Meditation**.

Our means of "*finding*" comes through meditation. (See Chapter 7)

These are the tools we are given.

What is the goal of our seeking? To "*improve conscious contact with God*."

The words in bold print below are the some of the tools we are given to help us understand Step 11 better:

Improve. *To get better*.

Conscious. ***Fully** awake, aware*. ("*I was asleep, dreaming I was awake*." Mark Houston)

Contact. *A connection between two separate entities through which energy passes between*.

Knowledge of His will for us. *To understand, comprehend with specificity*.

Power to carry that out. *Great or marked ability to do or act; power, strength*.

Chapter 3

THE PROBLEM

Step 11: *"Sought through prayer and meditation to improve our conscious contact with God as we understood Him, praying only for knowledge of His will for us and the power to carry that out."*

The Spiritual Malady

> *We have not only been mentally and physically ill, we have been spiritually sick. When the spiritual malady is overcome, we straighten out mentally and physically.*[22]

The Big Book gives us many pertinent examples of the problem:

> *For us, material well-being always **followed** spiritual progress; **it never preceded it**.*[23] *(*emphasis mine*)*

> *. . . a hopeless condition of mind and body.*[24]

---

[22] *Alcoholics Anonymous,* p. 64.

[23] *Ibid.,* p. 20.

[24] *Ibid.,* p. 20.

Fred would not . . . accept a spiritual remedy for his problem.[25]

Much of the "Doctor's Opinion" focuses on having a spiritual experience as the only remedy for our condition.

. . . other methods failed completely[26]

What are some of the "other methods?" Diet, exercise, counseling, material accumulation, etc.

Unless this person can experience an entire psychic change (that is, spiritual, mental, physical), there is very little hope of his recovery.[27]

. . .

One feels something more than human power is needed to produce the essential psychic change.[28]

Understanding How We're Made

The following picture illustrates what page 64 of the Big Book describes. We like to say, "It's an inside job," and that's true. First, we become connected, or

---

[25] *Ibid.*, p. 39.

[26] *Ibid.*, p. xxv.

[27] *Ibid.*, p. xxix.

[28] *Ibid.*, p. xxix.

surrendered to God in our human spirit, and God begins to work there—from the *inside out*.

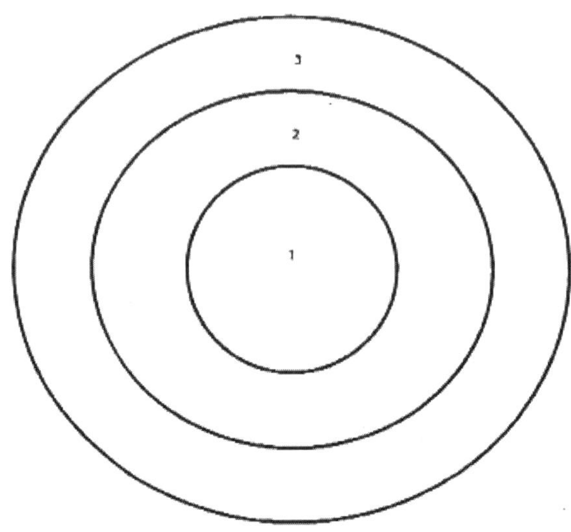

Spiritual Health.

The inner circle (1) represents the spirit in each of us. Bill refers to it as "*the heart*" in the Big Book. Others refer to it as the "center," or the "seat of power." At some point, it is believed that when we invite God in, our spirit is ignited and made alive, by His Spirit.

> *The central fact of our lives today is the absolute certainty that our Creator* ***has*** *(past tense) entered into* ***our hearts*** *and lives (present tense) in a way which is indeed miraculous.*[29]

[29] *Ibid.*, p. 25.

How did this happen, and when did it happen? Was it always there? Though many feel the Big Book is unclear, in Bill's Story he says the power that was keeping Ebby T. sober had not originated **in him**. (Ebby)[30]

You may be asking yourself, "why is this important?"

When I am unconnected to God, I'm living on will power alone and without God's point of view or power. We are limited to self-knowledge, and where addiction to alcohol/drugs, etc., is concerned, that's never enough.

Before he achieved permanent sobriety, Bill W. made this mistake. He thought he could somehow obtain sufficient **knowledge** to overcome his alcoholic problem.

> *Surely this was the answer—**self-knowledge . . . but it was not.***[31]

Throughout the Big Book, Bill uses other examples:

> *But the actual or potential alcoholic, with hardly an exception, will be absolutely unable*

[30] *Ibid.*, p. 11.

[31] *Ibid.*, p. 7.

to stop drinking on the ***basis of self-knowledge****.*[32]

Above all, he believed he had acquired such a profound ***knowledge*** *of the inner workings of his mind and its hidden springs that relapse was unthinkable.*[33]

He had much ***knowledge*** *about himself as an alcoholic. Yet all reasons for not drinking were easily pushed aside . . .*[34]

We could will these things with all our might, but the needed power wasn't there.[35]

. . . however deep his faith and ***knowledge****, he could not have applied it or he would not drink.*[36]

He was positive that . . . the ***knowledge*** *he had acquired, would keep him sober the rest of his life.* ***Self-knowledge*** *would fix it.*[37]

I saw that will power and ***self-knowledge*** *would not help in those strange mental blank spots.*[38]

---

[32] *Ibid.*, p. 39.

[33] *Ibid.*, p. 26.

[34] *Ibid.*, p. 37.

[35] *Ibid.*, p. 45.

[36] *Ibid.*, p. 93.

[37] *Ibid.*, p. 40.

So, I cannot get smart enough for victory over my addiction. Nor can I contact God through knowledge. I must have an *experience.*

However, once connected to the source of ALL power, we can receive limitless inspiration and spiritual power.

> *Much has already been said about receiving strength, inspiration, and direction from Him who has* **ALL KNOWLEDGE AND POWER**. *If we have carefully followed directions, we have begun to sense the flow of His Spirit into us. To some extent, we have become God-conscious. We have begun to develop this vital sixth sense.*[39] (emphasis mine)

Once connected to God, and having initially had the major obstacles removed that blocked us through doing the 12 steps, we can daily ask God to "direct our **THINKING**, especially asking that it be divorced from self-pity, dishonest or self-seeking motives. Under **THESE CONDITIONS** [turning our thinking over to God, freed of wrong motives], we can **EMPLOY OUR MENTAL FACULTIES WITH ASSURANCE**, for after all, God gave us brains to use." Thus, our mental faculties, which once produced only impotence, become useful, surrendered to God's known will.

---

[38] *Ibid.*, p. 42.

[39] *Ibid.*, p. 85

We now have a way to test our new thinking,*"by the new God-consciousness within."*[40]

> *Had this power originated in him? Obviously, it had not. There had been (past tense) no more power in him than there was in me at that minute (present tense); and that was none at all.*[41]

Many believe that at some point, perhaps in the First or Third Step, we surrender and God comes in.[42] This may be easier than some may think.

> *We found that God does not make too hard terms with those who seek Him.*[43]

Each one must decide the details based on individual understanding, and subsequent experience. As important as **when** God comes in, it is more important **that** God comes in, and is welcomed. We begin, with our own "conception" of God. Conception means "beginning." Our understanding grows from there.

---

[40] *Ibid.*, p. 13.

[41] *Ibid.*, p. 11.

[42] Some believe p. 55 says God is already there. A closer examination of the text indicates that what *is* there is the "*fundamental **idea** of God*." That is, God exists, and he is absent from my life. He is "*other-than*," or separate from me. We hear many describe this absence as the *"God –shaped hole."* I'll leave this argument up to theologians.

[43] *Ibid.*, p. 46.

Much spiritual literature indicates the human spirit has three functions in relationship to knowing God:

a. Conscience
b. Communion
c. Intuition

This is where my newly-awakened spirit knows God—in spirit. We have entered this world!

Thus, we are given a new basis for God's influence upon our thinking: the "*new God-consciousness within*."[44]

If you haven't found this new God consciousness, then you may **not** be who you think you are. You are not the sum total of your accomplishments—or failures. But when we don't truly know God, he'll look a lot like us. We'll make Him up.

We also discover that God cannot be reached with our intellect. No matter how much we know **about** God, it is not the same thing as **knowing** God. The "*new God-consciousness within*" lives in my spirit (Circle #1)

[44] *Ibid.*, p. 13.

Mental Health.

The middle circle (2) represents other areas affected by our new surrender to God. This mental area also consists of three parts:

1. The mind
2. The emotions
3. The will

These areas may also be referred to as your thinker, your feeler, and your chooser. Mystics call it the "soul" of a human. Many times we've heard it said from someone new who is describing bad choices in relationships that: *"My picker is broke."* That's the will. God can heal the way I think, which controls the way I feel, and influences the choices I make. This book is about the part I play in this transformation.

> *We, who have recovered from serious drinking, are miracles of mental health*.[45]

Again, the mental covers these three areas. As we make progress we discover the battle is for the mind, and the prize is the will—our "picker."

The Body.

The outer circle (3) represents the body. As we begin to put *"first things first"* and start to heal spiritually, this trickles down (or **out**, using our three

[45] *Ibid.*, p. 133.

circles), to affect the realms of mental faculties **and** the physical body. As the Big Book says:

> *We are convinced that a spiritual mode of living is a most powerful health restorative.*[46]

Some believe that we are only spiritual beings and all we need to focus on is the spiritual life. This, however, seems inconsistent with what we read in the Big Book. We need a healthy mind, will, emotions and body to be complete and fully perform the "*role God has assigned*." How much good would we be if our body was run down, even though our spirit was functioning well? Page 133 also urges us to stay in good health by using the gifts God has given us, such as "*doctors, psychologists, and practitioners of various kinds*."[47]

NOTES:

____

____

____

____

____

____

---

[46] *Ibid.*, p. 133.

[47] *Ibid.*, p. 133.

Chapter 4

The Solution

A Closer Look at Pages 86-88

Step 11 suggests prayer and meditation. We shouldn't be shy on this matter of prayer. Better men than we are using it CONSTANTLY. It works, if we have the proper attitude and work at it. It would be easy to be vague about this matter. Yet, we believe we can make some definite and valuable suggestions.[48] (emphasis mine)

In this paragraph, a few things stand out. One, if we want the benefits promised, we must do certain things *"constantly,"* with regularity.

Secondly, there are directions to follow! The word *"if"* lets us know a **condition** exists. That is, **if** I do **this**, I will get **that.**

Here are the conditions we must apply for success with prayer and meditation:

(a) Have **the proper attitude**, and

[48] *Ibid.*, pp. 85-86.

(b) **Work at it**. No one does this perfectly, but we continue to work on it and make progress as we do.

We next read that it is *"easy to be vague about this matter"* (prayer and meditation). For instance, I can't have a "*whatever*" approach; "it doesn't matter what I do as long as I do **something**." This is simply not true. There are specific suggestions that have been helpful for millions. "*We believe we can make some* <u>*definite*</u> *and valuable suggestions."*

> *On awakening, let us think about the 24 hours ahead. We consider our plans for the day. Before we begin, we* ***ask God*** *to direct our thinking, especially* ***asking*** *that it be divorced from self-pity, dishonest, or self-seeking motives. Under these conditions we can employ our mental faculties with assurance, for after all God gave us brains to use. Our thought-life will be placed on a much higher plane when our thinking is clear of wrong motives.*
>
> *In thinking about our day, we may face indecision. We may not be able to determine which course to take. Here we* ***ask God*** *for inspiration, an intuitive thought or a decision. We relax and take it easy. We don't struggle. We are often surprised how the right answers come after we have tried this for a while. What used to be the hunch or the occasional inspiration gradually becomes a working part*

of the mind. Being still inexperienced, and having just made conscious contact with God, it is not probable we are going to be inspired at all times. We might pay for this presumption in all sorts of absurd actions and ideas. Nevertheless, we find that our thinking will, as time passes, be more and more on the plane of inspiration. We come to rely upon it.

*We usually conclude the period of meditation with a prayer [**asking**] that we be shown all through the day what our next step is to be, that we be given whatever we need to take care of such problems. We **ask** especially for freedom from self-will, and are careful to make no requests for ourselves only. We may **ask** for ourselves, however, if other will be helped. We are careful never to pray for our own selfish ends. Many of us have wasted a lot of time doing that and it doesn't work. You can easily see why.*

Prayer: 85-88. Asking, not demanding. Eleven "asks" in Step 11.

Why would we be directed to "*ask*" if there were no possibility of hearing or receiving "answers"? Would I encourage my children to ask questions, only to refuse to answer them?

Here are some definitions of important words/phrases from pages 86-88.

- **Often**: Frequently, many times at short intervals
- **Surprised**: A sudden feeling of wonder or astonishment, as through unexpectedness

- "***An intuitive thought***." Direct perception of truth **independent of any reasoning process**; **immediate** apprehension. Keen, quick insight; pure, untaught, non-inferential knowledge. The act of knowing **without the use of rational processes**; immediate cognition; a sense of something not evident or deductible; an **impression**.

- "***Intuitive decision***." An answer, a resolution to a question. One based on **instinctive knowing**, an "***impression***." *"He had an intuition that something had gone wrong."*

> *"Intuition is the ally of reason."* John Kagleman
>
> *"(Intuition is) the extra sensory perception of reality."* Alexis Carrel

- "***Inspiration***." Defined as "divine guidance or influence directly and immediately exerted upon the mind or soul. Arousal of the mind to special, unusual activity. **A sudden intuition as part of solving a problem** (e.g., pictures, thoughts, words).

- "***Hunch***." A premonition or suspicion; guess.

- "***Conscious contact***."

a. Conscious: fully aware, awake; (a certain) knowing; immediate proximity.

b. Contact: *"A junction of electrical conductors that controls current or flow [of power], often completing or interrupting a current."*

- *"Gradually becomes a working part of the mind."* (The new God-consciousness within, pp. 13, 85.)

- *"**Excitement**."* (p. 88) Agitated, frantic, panic.

NOTES:

____

____

____

____

____

Chapter 5

SEEKING

Step 11: *"SOUGHT through prayer and meditation to improve our conscious contact with God as we understood Him, praying only for knowledge of His will for us, and the power to carry that out."*

> *Faith is a living, daring confidence in God's grace, so sure and certain that a man could stake his life on it a thousand times.* Martin Luther

This brief chapter describes seeking. Like we often hear, recovery is a process of taking action and discovering results. In this specific sense, we discover that we **see** God (or find God), when we **seek** God.

Yes, sometimes God surprises us, and just breaks in. But the regular practice of taking time each morning to open our hearts to pray, meditate, listen, and write will most often provide the best results. I want to find a way to give God room each day to "*build with me and do with me as [He] wants.*"

Seeking is similar to preparing a construction site for a building. First, the foundation must be dug; then, the forms created for the concrete to fill in. Our morning practice provides the form—opening of the heart—for God to come and fill in.

We "*made a decision*" in Step 3 to turn our wills and lives over to the care of God; seeking God is the practical demonstration of our continuing to practice this decision.

NOTES:

Chapter 6

PRAYER

Step 11: *"Sought through PRAYER and meditation to improve our conscious contact with God as we understood Him, praying only for knowledge of His will for us, and the power to carry that out."*

> *Grant that I may not pray alone with the mouth; help me that I may pray from the depths of my heart.* Martin Luther

> *Faith is a living, daring confidence in God's grace, so sure and certain that a man could stake his life on it a thousand times.* Martin Luther

> *Courage is fear that has said its prayers.* Dorothy Bernard

How Do We Pray?

What makes prayer work? If I'm just **saying** words, I'm wasting my breath. On pages 86-88 there are at least 11 "*asks*." Why would the Big Book direct me to ask, if I think I won't receive an answer? Most people don't enjoy just "*going through the motions*." The action of **intentional** prayer is called **faith**.

1. FAITH is confidence in God, because I am coming to know that God is good.
2. FAITH says "*thank you*" after asking.
3. FAITH is being sure of what we hope for and certain of what we do not see.
4. FAITH is the assurance (the confirmation of) the things (we) hope for, being the proof of things (we) do not see, and the conviction of their reality (faith) perceiving as real fact what is not revealed to the senses.
5. FAITH is spelled R.I.S.K.

We begin with the end in mind: "***knowledge of His will, power to carry that out***." What is His will for me? If I know his will, I can pray with more confidence.

The following are some steps I take when I pray:

1. I wait in God's presence and get comfortable.
2. I consider what God's will for me might be.
3. I ask God for HIS faith to pray with confidence
4. I ask God to act.
5. I say "*thank you*."

6. Our prayers and our *"after"* conversation need to be consistent. I must not pray one thing, and then say something else that is inconsistent with my prayer.
7. I turn my attention to what God would have me be, or who I can help.

On page 86, it says when uncertain we *"ask God..."* and then we *"relax and take it easy."* That's faith. If I can't relax, did I really trust God?

Faith can pray this way, because when I have faith, I know that God will answer my prayers.

Prayer:

- As a means of **improving** my conscious contact;
- As a means of **exercising** *"God consciousness"* (p. 85);
- As a means of **doing** His will;
- As a means of **bringing** God's will into my world;
- As a means of **becoming** of maximum service to God and our fellows.

Principles are not Presence. The 12 steps are a set of principles. However, the goal is to have conscious contact with God. Principles keep me from going in the ditch when I can't find His presence. His presence is consistent with these 12 principles but

Presence can bring me more specific, pertinent, personal guidance.

***Saying* Prayers Versus *Praying* Prayers**

Here is a story that may help explain the difference between saying prayers and praying prayers.

When I was young, I belonged to a church where the regular confession of sins was mandatory. This practice had always been difficult for me because I didn't like following rules set by anyone, let alone by a church that I wasn't quite sure I believed in. I felt a growing need to reject the whole God idea, but I wasn't quite ready. I was still afraid of the possible fiery consequences of sin not confessed.

After I started middle school, my friends and I learned that a certain young girl would allow boys to take some rather tame liberties with her. As soon as we heard about it, we secretly planned to meet with her on a Saturday afternoon—just before confession time. After the deed was done, we ran to church and got in the confessional line. All too quickly, it was my turn to go in and tell all to the priest. I gathered all my courage and told him what I had done. After what seemed like an eternity, he instructed me never to repeat the sin and to immediately say 100 "*Hail Marys*" and 50 "*Our Fathers*."

I sank into the nearest pew and, using nothing but rote memory, said the prayers to myself as fast as I could. I didn't think about anything except keeping track of the numbers. I wanted to be forgiven and leave as fast as possible. After all, it was Saturday, and I had things to do!

Those prayers had no meaning for me. I was *saying* prayers, not *praying* prayers.

Now I'm on a different spiritual path with God. I am coming to understand and beginning to experience how unconditionally I am loved. Now, I practice the art of *praying* my prayers.

My words to God these days are intentional, thoughtful, and passionate. I *mean* what I pray. If I now find myself at the end (or middle) of a prayer like The Serenity Prayer and realize my mind has wandered, I go back to the beginning and start over. I am making conscious contact with God, and know I am being heard.

SO, LET'S PRACTICE. Wait. Listen. Ask for faith. Ask. Thank him.

MEDITATION

Step 11: *"Sought through prayer and MEDITATION to improve our conscious contact with God as we understood Him, praying only for knowledge of His will for us, and the power to carry that out."*

How Do We Meditate?

> *Meditation is something which can always be further developed. It has no boundaries, of width or height or depth. Aided by such instruction and example as we can find, it is essentially an individual adventure, something which each one of us works out in his own way. But its object is always the same: to improve our conscious contact with God, with His grace, wisdom, and love.*[49]

What **is** meditation?

One ancient language translates the word for meditation "*to mutter*." This changed the way I viewed folks walking on the street, talking to themselves. Maybe they weren't crazy—maybe they were meditating!

---

[49] *Twelve Steps and Twelve Traditions,* pp. 101-102.

Some definitions of the word meditation:

- To reflect deeply on a subject;
- To think intently and at length, as for spiritual purposes;
- To keep the mind in a state of contemplation; to dwell on anything in thought; to think seriously; to muse; to cogitate; to reflect.

One idea from this passage in *Twelve Steps and Twelve Traditions* to keep in mind is that it suggests the goal, and a practical way to measure our progress if what we're doing is working. Is it serving to "*improve our conscious contact with God, with His grace, wisdom and love*"?

In other words, no matter *how* I'm practicing meditation is it—

- Improving my conscious contact with God? Am I feeling more connected today, than last week? Last month? Last year? Am I hearing more clearly from God than I have in the past?
- Improving my contact with God's *grace* (divine empowerment)?
- Improving my contact with God's *wisdom*?
- Improving my contact with God's *love*?

Some believe that spiritual growth cannot be measured. In AA (or whatever your 12-step affiliation may be) it's easy to live "*in the world of spiritual make believe*."[50] Often, some of the most difficult people to get along with "in recovery," are those who call themselves spiritual. They may also be self-righteous and angry. "*No one understands me! Just God! I must run the entire universe all by myself!*"

If we cannot love our fellows whom we *can* see, do we really love God, whom we *cannot* see?

It may surprise you to know Bill Wilson said spiritual growth **can** be measured. Our motives when we pray may or may not be judged "*spiritual*," but others can observe the "*fruits*" (results or changes) in our lives. Are we more peaceful, loving, and tolerant today than we used to be? As someone remarked, "*If it's spiritual, it's practical*."

Near the end of Chapter 5, "How it Works," we read, "*The principles we have set down are **guides** to progress*." A guide can help us measure the distance we've traveled. Are we closer to God and His grace, wisdom, and love? If not, perhaps we should reevaluate our meditation practice.

Many of us have tried various forms of meditation. The example used in *Twelve Steps and Twelve Traditions* is an ancient spiritual practice and one I have been using for 40 years. This method of

---

[50] *Alcoholics Anonymous,* p. 130.

meditation suggests that we focus on a phrase or inspirational saying that seems to be true, or we HOPE it is! The book *Twelve Steps and Twelve Traditions* uses the St. Francis Prayer as an example. Let's think of the first line of that prayer: "*Lord, make me an instrument of your peace.*" Try saying this phrase over and over, thinking about what each word means to you.[51] While repeating the phrase, emphasize a different word each time. Perhaps you will want to look up the word's definition. By doing this, while meditating on the first part of the Serenity Prayer, I learned that "serenity" means "a peaceful state of untroubled calm."

Will you stop right now, and try this for, say, five minutes?

> **LORD** (or God), make me an instrument of your peace (repeat 3-4 times);
>
> Lord, **MAKE** me an instrument of your peace (repeat emphasis 3-4 times);
>
> Lord, make **ME** an instrument of your peace;
>
> Lord, make me **AN** instrument of your peace;
>
> Lord, make me an **INSTRUMENT** of your peace;
>
> Lord, make me an instrument **OF** your peace;
>
> Lord, make me an instrument of **YOUR** peace;

---

[51] The Big Book says, we set aside our prejudice(s) against spiritual terms and ask ourselves what they mean to us.

Lord, make me an instrument of your **PEACE**.

Some of the things that come to mind when I am meditating on this particular prayer are thus:

LORD = God; all knowing; benevolent; kind; tender; all powerful, etc.

MAKE = create; transform; fashion; shape.

ME = my life; my heart; my motivations

AN = one of many; one instrument in a symphony

INSTRUMENT = I picture which one I might be: strings? woodwinds?

OF = out from, through

YOUR = Yours, God, not mine

PEACE = Serenity, comfort, harmony, calm

Many have told me when it was suggested they join our daily group for meditation, that they couldn't possibly quiet their mind for five minutes! I happily told them that they don't have to do that. We are engaging our minds as we use this practice, not dis-engaging it. Just this week, I introduced this approach to two new "*meditators*." When five minutes was up, they could not believe the time had gone by so fast! The proof is in the pudding, as they say. Both meditators felt more connected to God and more peaceful after just five minutes! Often, a feeling of "intoxication" results. This feeling is actually a promise found on page 128 of the Big Book, which says, "*We have indulged in spiritual intoxication*." What we were looking for all along in the drink or the drug, is available to us, and we discover we "*like the effects produced by*" . . . meditation.

We discover many of us are already meditating, but don't realize it. If I asked you, "What is 2 times 4?" you would probably answer without hesitation, 8! If I told you that I didn't see you counting on your fingers before you answered, you'd probably tell me it's because you know it by heart. Ah, yes; but you *learned* it by mouth. That's meditation. My mom used flash cards to help me memorize my multiplication tables. I repeated them over and over until I knew them "by heart." After a while, I internalized the truth of "2 times 4 equals 8."

When we find things we want to internalize, we focus on them, and over time, they become a part of us. This is true in the negative as well as the positive.

Another example I like to use is to describe the way cows digest grass. A cow has four stomach compartments. A cow bends over, chomps on a hunk of grass, and then swallows it. Next, it regurgitates it. (Thank you God, you didn't make us that way! The cow then chews on the regurgitated grass some more, and swallows it again. It spits it up, then chews it some more. Cows continue this process until **what it's chewing on is fully digested**. That's meditation.[52] Meditate on a truth until you cannot be persuaded otherwise. Or, as I often say, until you "*know in your knower*." Once there, it cannot be taken from you.

Here are some other words to meditate on with their definitions. Why not stop right now and try one for five minutes? Then, do it every day, or several times a day, for one week.

Sample Meditations

"God, give me . . .

1. **Serenity"** (Peaceful, untroubled calm)
2. **Courage**" (The ability to face and deal with anything—difficult, dangerous, or painful, without retreating.) This is a great one to repeat when doing a 4th step, or just before an amends.
3. **Wisdom**" (Sound judgment). "*God, give me wisdom; sound judgment*." Because timing is everything!

---

[52] One morning, while explaining this to a new person, the light went on. "That's it!" she exclaimed. "I'm trying to swallow things (truths) before they're fully digested!"

Another method to try is to use the breath as a cue for a phrase. For example:

Breathe in: *"The love of God fills me."*

Breathe out: *"The grace of God surrounds me."*

Chapter 8

IMPROVING CONSCIOUS CONTACT

Step 11: *"Sought through prayer and meditation to IMPROVE OUR CONSCIOUS CONTACT WITH GOD as we understood Him, praying only for knowledge of His will for us, and the power to carry that out."*

To **improve** something implies that we already have a measure of it, and we are trying to make it better, gain more.

As defined in Chapter 4, **conscious** means fully aware, awake; [a certain] knowing; immediate proximity.

Contact means: *"A junction of electrical conductors that controls current or flow [of power], often completing or interrupting a current."*

When we are connected to power, we know it! Once, I accidently stuck my hand into a "live" electrical wire. There was no doubt that I had made contact with a power greater than myself!

This isn't something we can make up or manufacture; but, if we practice prayer and meditation, we will wake up to a new flow of power—God's power.

This new way of seeing can take many forms. Some literally **hear** God speak to them; some **get a distinct impression** of God speaking to them; some may see a **picture** in the mind, or a **sense** of what God is trying to communicate. Regardless of **how** you hear God, each one that *"has honestly tried this"* comes to hear God in the unique way that God has made you to hear. A later chapter explains how we can measure such hearing, and Chapter 11, "How to Listen to God" directs us to share what we hear with another trusted friend when we are in doubt.

NOTES:

____

____

____

____

____

____

____

____

Chapter 9

KNOWLEDGE OF HIS WILL

Step 11: *"Sought through prayer and meditation to improve our conscious contact with God as we understood Him, praying only for KNOWLEDGE OF HIS WILL FOR US, and the power to carry that out."*

> *Everyone has his own specific vocation or mission in life; everyone must carry out a concrete assignment that demands fulfillment. Therein he cannot be replaced, nor can his life be repeated, thus, everyone's task is unique as his specific opportunity to implement it.*
> **Viktor E. Frankl**

Many times, I've heard AA members declare we cannot know the will of God, since God, being infinite and all powerful, is unknowable. Therefore, we cannot understand God **or** His specific will. This belief often creates false ideas such as, "*If it's supposed to happen, it will happen,*" and "*Whatever happens must be God's will.*" This type of thinking results in a passive acceptance of whatever life happens to throw our way. This sounds a lot like victimhood. I believe these views are inconsistent with AA literature and history.

The question is: Why would I be directed to seek both God **and** His will if it were not knowable, or attainable? Would you expect your children, friends, or co-workers to guess what we expect from them?

There are at least 18 passages in the Big Book that refer to seeking guidance from God. Here are two:

> *. . . so we clean house with the family, asking each morning in meditation that our Creator* ***show us*** *the way of patience, tolerance, kindliness and love.*[53]

And again:

> *. . . I was to sit quietly when in doubt,* ***asking only for direction*** *and strength* ***to meet my problems as He would have me.***[54]

The following is a fun, easy exercise that may help you to discover how much you already know about the will of God. I'm convinced we can open the Big Book to **any page** and find a promise for us within. A promise is an *absolute guarantee*. For example, "*I promise if you read this book and practice these exercises, you will improve your conscious contact with God*!" A promise **to us** is the will of God **for us**. So, take out a blank sheet of paper or use the form below and write at the top:

---

[53] *Ibid.*, p. 83.

[54] *Ibid.*, p. 13.

THE WILL OF GOD FOR ME IS:

Then, as fast as you can, write one or two words per line. Write what you KNOW to be the absolute will of God for you.

____

____

____

____

____

____

____

____

____

____

Usually, within five minutes the average person has from five to twenty-five items and is surprised they knew so many!

An obvious one to start with is THE WILL OF GOD FOR ME IS:

Sobriety.

Do you believe sobriety is God's will for you? If not, you probably won't stay sober! "*There is ONE who has all power—that one is God. May you find him now*!" I know God is bigger than me, so whatever God wants, God makes happen. I'm convinced He wants me sober. (Everyone else in my family sure does!)

I find it curious to hear so many AA members say, in anticipation of a sobriety birthday, "*God willing, I'll have _____ years next month*." It sounds sort of pseudo-humble, but it's really not. Of course God is willing! Otherwise, all of my self-will, and self-effort would fail.

Now, at the bottom of your sheet of paper, write, "*YOU ARE MY* ______________________." Finish the sentence with one desired promise from your list of the things you believe God wills for you to have. For instance, if "*love*" is on your list, try meditating on "*You (God) are my ability to love*."

This style of meditation focuses on the source (God) and the present (*are*). So, when we say you **are** my ___________, I'm bringing God into the present moment to provide this for me. I'll say, "*You **are**, not were, or will be some day, but **right now***!"

Below, you will find **49** additional items for your list, condensed into three paragraphs.

The "*promises*" on page 63, first paragraph contain **16**;

The "*promises*," on pages 83-84 contain **19**;

The paragraph beginning on page 84 "And we have ceased fighting" contains **14**.

Go on a treasure hunt and see how many YOU can find!

NOTES:

Chapter 10

THE POWER TO CARRY THAT OUT

Step 11: *"Sought through prayer and meditation to improve our conscious contact with God as we understood Him, praying only for knowledge of His will for us, and the POWER TO CARRY THAT OUT."*

As stated at the beginning, on page 5 of this book, *"Lack of power"* is our common dilemma. We seek God in Step 11, not only to find His will for our lives, but to equip us with the power to *do* His will. What good would it be, for instance, if you sent me to the hardware store to buy lumber, but gave me no money? Even if I come to know what God's will is for me, I still need God's power to accomplish it. If your dream, your goals, those things you *know in your knower* to be the will of God for you can be accomplished by your human resources alone, I doubt if it's big enough to be God.

Just today, someone texted me these words: "*It takes more than bread to stay alive. It takes a steady stream of words from God's mouth*." Now that I am beginning to sense what God wants for me and for my life, I can trust that He is also giving me His power to accomplish that will. As someone wisely said, "*What God orders, God pays for*." So, if God directs you to do anything because it's his will for you, the resources will become available. What does the Big Book tell us about access to this Power?

> *Being all powerful, He provided what we needed, if we kept close to Him. . .*[55]

> *As we felt new* ***power*** *flow in . . . we began to lose our fear. . . .*[56]

> *[T]hey found that a new power . . . flowed into them.*[57]

NOTES:

____

____

____

____

____

____

____

____

[55] *Ibid.*, p. 63.

[56] *Ibid.*, p. 63.

[57] Ibid. p. 83

Chapter 11

HOW TO LISTEN TO GOD

[I received the following instructions on "listening prayer" from Wally P., the archivist for Dr. Bob's papers. He discovered that Dr. Bob brought this helpful exercise into early AA from the Oxford Group.[58] *The exercise was written by John Batterson. What I have discovered, with hundreds and hundreds of people I've shared them with, is that it works!]*

Below are a few simple ideas and suggestions for people who are willing to try an experiment. You can discover for yourself the most important and practical thing any human being can ever learn—how to be in touch with God.

All that is needed is the **willingness to try it honestly**. Every person who has done this consistently and sincerely has found that it really works. Before you begin, look over these fundamental points. They are true and are based on the experience of thousands of people.

1. God is alive. He always has been and He always will be.

[58] The Oxford Group was a spiritual movement that grew rapidly in the United States and abroad. It was founded by Frank Buchmann, following a spiritual experience he had in Wales, around 1904.

2. God knows everything.
3. God can do anything.
4. God can be everywhere—all at the same time. (These are the important differences between God and human beings.)
5. God is invisible. We can't see Him or touch Him, but **God is here**. He is with you now. He is beside you. He fills the room or the place where you are right now.
6. God cares very much for **you**. He has an answer for every need and problem you face.
7. God will tell you all that you **need** to know. He will not always tell you all that you **want** to know.
8. God will help you do anything that He asks you to do.
9. Anyone can be in touch with God, anywhere and at any time, **if the conditions are obeyed.**

These are the conditions:

- Be quiet and still
- Listen
- Be honest about every thought that comes
- Test the thoughts to be sure that they come from God
- Follow the direction received

With these basic elements as a background, here are specific suggestions on *How to Listen to God:*

1. Take Time

Find a place and time where you can be alone, quiet, and undisturbed. Most people have found that early morning is the best time. Get some paper and a pen or pencil.

2. Relax

Sit in a comfortable position. Consciously relax all your muscles. Be loose. Tell yourself there is no hurry. There should be no strain during these minutes. God cannot get through as easily if we are tense and anxious about later responsibilities.

3. Tune In

Open your heart to God. Either silently or aloud, talk to God in a natural way and tell him that you would like to find His plan for your life, your destiny, and how you may be useful today. You could also ask Him for an answer to a problem or situation that you are facing. Be definite and specific with your request.

4. Listen

Be still, quiet, relaxed, and open. Let God do the talking. Thoughts, ideas, and impressions will begin to come into your mind and heart. Be alert, aware, and open to whatever you are hearing or sensing.

5. Write!

This is the key to the whole process. Write down everything that comes into your mind. **Everything!** Writing is simply a means of recording whatever you receive from God so that that you can remember it later. **Don't** sort out or edit your thoughts at this point.

Try not to say to yourself:

- This thought isn't important
- This is just an ordinary thought
- This can't be guidance
- This isn't nice
- This can't be from God
- This is just me thinking . . . etc.

Write down everything that passes through your mind:

- Names of people
- Things to do
- Things to say
- Things that are wrong and need to be made right

Write down everything:

- Good thoughts/Bad thoughts
- Comfortable thoughts/Uncomfortable thoughts
- "*Holy*" thoughts/"*Unholy*" thoughts
- Sensible thoughts/Insane thoughts

Be honest! Write down **everything**! A thought comes quickly, and it escapes even more quickly unless it is captured and written down.

6. Test

When the flow of thoughts slows down, stop writing. Take a good look at what you have written. Not every thought we have comes from God, so we consider what we've written. Here is where the written record helps us to be able to look at our thoughts.

a. Are these thoughts completely honest, pure, unselfish, and loving?

b. Are these thoughts consistent with what we believe to be the will of God?

c. Are these thoughts in line with our understanding of the teachings found in our spiritual literature?

7. Check

When in doubt, what do you think another person who is living two-way prayer would think about this thought or action? More light comes in through two windows than one. Someone else who also wants God's plan for our lives may help us to see more clearly.

Talk to others about what you have written. Many people do this. They tell each other what guidance has come. This is the secret of unity. Guidance shows us what is right, not who is right.

8. Follow Through

Do what you are guided to do. You will only be sure of guidance as you do it. A rudder will not guide a boat unless the boat is moving. As you obey the direction you receive, very often you will discover that the results of your actions will convince you that you are on the right track.

9. Blocks

What if we don't seem to get any definite thoughts? Look at the following possibilities. Remember, God's guidance is as freely available as the air we breathe.

Usually, it is because there is something **I will not do**:

- There may be something wrong in my life that I will not face and make right
- There may be a habit or indulgence I will not give up
- There may be a person I will not forgive
- There may be a wrong relationship in my life
- There may be an amends I will not make
- There may be something God has already told me to do that I refuse to do

Begin taking these actions and try listening again.

10. Mistakes

Suppose I make a mistake; of course we all make mistakes. We are humans with many faults. However, God will always honor our sincerity.

God will work around and through every honest mistake we make. He will help us make it right. But, remember this: sometimes when we do obey God, someone else may not like it or agree with it. So when there is opposition, it doesn't always mean you have made a mistake. It can mean that the other person doesn't want to know or to do what is right!

Suppose I fail to do something that I have been directed to do and the opportunity to do it passes? There is only one thing to do. Put it right with God. Tell Him you're sorry. Ask Him to forgive you, then accept His forgiveness and begin again. God is our father—He is not an impersonal calculator. He understands us far better than we understand ourselves.

11. Results

We never know what swimming is like until we get down into the water and try. We will never know what this is like until we sincerely try it.

Every person who has tried this honestly finds that a wisdom, not their own, comes **into their minds** and that a Power greater than human power begins to operate in their lives. It is an endless adventure.

There is a way of life, for everyone, everywhere. Anyone can be in touch with the living God, anywhere, anytime, **if we fulfill His conditions**. This is the law of prayer.

When man listens, God speaks
When man obeys, God acts.

<u>This is the law of prayer.</u>

God's plan for this world goes forward through the lives of ordinary people who are willing to be guided by Him.

NOTES:

____

____

____

____

____

____

____

Chapter 12

WHEN WE RETIRE AT NIGHT

Every evening I turn my worries over to God. He's going to be up all night anyway.

Mary C. Crowley

When we retire at night, we constructively review our day. Were we resentful, selfish, dishonest or afraid? Do we owe an apology? Have we kept something to ourselves which should be discussed with another person at once? Were we kind and loving toward all? What could we have done better? Were we thinking of ourselves most of the time? Or were we thinking of what we could do for others, of what we could pack into the stream of life? But we must be careful not to drift into worry, remorse, or morbid reflection, for that would diminish our usefulness to others. After making our review, we ask God's forgiveness and inquire what corrective measures should be taken.[59]

The writer asks us 10 questions useful in reviewing our day:

[59] *Alcoholics Anonymous*, p. 86.

1. Was I resentful?
2. Was I selfish?
3. Was I dishonest
4. Was I afraid?
5. Do I owe an apology?
6. Have I kept something to myself which should be discussed with another person at once?
7. Was I kind and loving toward all?
8. What could I have done better?
9. Was I thinking of myself most of the time?
10. Was I thinking of what we could do for others, of what we could pack into the stream of life?

As we review our day, we are cautioned to beware of certain negative attitudes that may arise during this review.

> *But we must be careful not to drift into worry, remorse, or morbid reflection, for that would diminish our usefulness to others.*[60]

[60] *Ibid., p. 86.*

Then, after honestly reviewing our day, we are instructed:

> *After making our review, we* ***ask God's forgiveness*** *and inquire what corrective measures should be taken.*[61]

Killing the Bookkeeper.

I call this nightly exercise, "killing the bookkeeper." I want to deal with any negative baggage I might otherwise carry over into the next day if I ignore this valuable time. I deal with it each night, and am free to sleep better, dream better, and awake more refreshed.

The following exercise may help us review our day honestly, and deal with any problems carefully. As a result, we don't end up carrying them into our dreams, disturbing our sleep, and waking with a full "*backpack*" from the day before. It gives us a way to get God's forgiveness if needed, and go to sleep with a clear conscience. Thus, in our review, if we find areas we fell short in during that day, pray the following, asking God's forgiveness, and clearing the slate:

> *God, I made mistakes today when I (list specifics that came up). I ask Your forgiveness. Now, I receive Your forgiveness, and I choose to forgive myself. Remember—*

[61] *Ibid., p. 86.*

forgiveness is a decision, not an emotion. Finally, I mark it in time. I receive Your forgiveness and I choose to forgive myself, at 10:27 (or whatever time I am making this declaration).

If you're a more visual person, perhaps you might want to create a form for your evening review, such as the following.[62]

NOTES:

____

____

____

____

____

____

____

[62] Interestingly, many refer to their "nightly review" as a function of the 10th Step. It is actually a part of the function in Step 11. Though clearer when reading the Big Book, where the 10th Step refers to the things we look for cropping up during the day, the nightly review is clearly at bedtime, and situated in Step 11. Why is this important? It's important because it seems to bring partnership with God into this activity, and the perspective of being part of something we do prayerfully matters.

WHEN WE RETIRE AT NIGHT WE CONSTRUCTIVELY REVIEW OUR DAY

Was I:	(Be specific)
Resentful?	
Selfish?	
Dishonest?	
Afraid?	

Do I owe an apology?	
Kept something to myself which should be discussed with another person at once??	
Was I kind and loving toward all?	
What could I have done better?	
Was I thinking of myself most of the time? (*Yes* or *No*)	
Did I think about what I could do for others? (*Yes* or *No*)	(Examples)
What I could pack into life today?	

Have I drifted into	(Be specific)
Worry?	
Remorse?	
Morbid Reflection?	

"After making our review, we ask God's forgiveness." (Sample prayer: *"God, I ask you to forgive me for the behavior you have revealed to me*

about today (be specific). Then pause and say, *"I receive your forgiveness right now, at* (look at a watch or clock) ______am/pm, *and I* ***choose*** *to forgive myself."* I have found it extremely helpful to "mark this" in time.

"God, what corrective measures should be taken"?

____

____

____

"Thank you, God. Goodnight."

One question about this practice intrigued me. Why does *"When we retire at night"* come before *"On awakening"*?

After some wrestling with it, I came to believe it's because **every day begins the night before** (12 midnight). If I do not review my day, take any necessary corrective action, and ask forgiveness from God for my mistakes, I'll carry them into my sleeping hours, my dream life, and into the next day.

Though not Jewish, I re-read the Jewish account of creation: *"And there was <u>evening</u> and there was <u>morning</u>, the first day"*. . . *"and there was <u>evening</u> and there was <u>morning</u>, the second day"* and continuing through all the days of creation.

Again, I'm not Jewish, nor a biblical scholar, but I find the parallel to the Big Book in this instance quite interesting. I've drawn the conclusion that there is a causal link, that God designed us to rest before labor. "*And God rested on the seventh day from all his work that he had done.*" Jews consider their Sabbath the first day of the week, as do many calendars. The implied meaning seems to be we need beneficial rest before productive work. Not "*killing my internal bookkeeper*" will inhibit meaningful rest.

Remember: Every day begins the night before.

NOTES:

____

____

____

____

____

____

____

____

____

____

Chapter 13

PUTTING IT ALL TOGETHER

Either by yourself or with a friend or two, you are ready to put it all together. The only way to get started is to *just do it!* Based on what you've read to this point, here's a way to start.

Sample Suggested Daily Prayer and Meditation

- Listen to 5-10 minutes of music that speaks to you about God, or relaxes you
- Have someone pray the Third Step Prayer and Set Aside Prayer
- Do a five minute meditation on a chosen focus
- Read pp. 86-88, from On awakening
- Do the "How to Listen to God" exercise (ask God what He wants to say to you today, who to pray for. I write, "God, what do you want me to know today?")
- Share your writing with one another (if doing alone, text, call, or email your writing)
- Close with prayer (Seventh Step, St. Francis, or any other of your choice)

- Sometimes, in the middle, someone may share a reading from AA literature or other selected meaningful writings

There! You've done it. If you do it alone, this will probably take about 30 minutes. I believe you'll come to see it's the best 30 minutes you could invest in yourself, and you'll come to the place where you won't want to "*leave home without it*!"

NOTES:

Chapter 14

GETTING STARTED

The real problem of the [spiritual] life comes where people do not usually look for it. It comes the very moment you wake up each morning. All your wishes and hopes for the day come rushing at you like wild animals. And the first job each morning consists simply in shoving them all back; in listening to that other voice, taking that other point of view, letting that other larger, stronger, quieter life come flowing in. ***C.S. Lewis***

Those who believe they believe in God, but without passion in the heart, without anguish of mind, without uncertainty, without doubt, and even at times without despair, believe only in the idea of God, and not God himself. ***Unamuno***

- **Begin with Some Basics.**
    - **90-in-90**. We often hear it advised when one is beginning recovery to set a goal of one meeting a day, or, as it is referred to more commonly, "*Do 90 in 90*"; that is, 90 meetings in 90 days. Similarly, it can be most helpful to begin with meditation

as we did our beginning sobriety: "*Do 90 (meditations) in 90 days*!"

- **Find a Friend to Join You.**

- ***"If circumstances warrant***." To begin with, we may not be able to have others join us. Sometimes our schedule makes this difficult, or we live in a rural area, or simply cannot find someone willing to join. Perhaps, however, we can find what some call an "*accountability partner*"—someone we can call, email, or text each day with our writing and share, getting encouragement. This is often very helpful in becoming consistent.

NOTES:

___

___

___

___

___

___

Chapter 15

MEASURING SUCCESS

Believe it or not, spiritual progress is measurable. Really? Page 60 of the Big Book says, "*The principles we have set down are guides to progress*." So, there is a guide, a way to measure the progress we are making (or not making). Bill W. said this:

> *Meditation is something which can always be further developed. It has no boundaries, either of width or height. Aided by such instruction and example as we can find, it is essentially an individual adventure, something which each one of us works out in his own way. But its object is always the same: to improve our conscious contact with God, with His grace, wisdom, and love.*[63]

Therefore, the first question we may ask ourselves honestly is "*Has my practice of these principles **improved** my conscious contact with God? Is my ability to know His will clearer to me than it was a month, a year, or five years ago*"? You might want

[63] *Twelve Steps and Twelve Traditions*, p. 101.

to ask yourself if you are more loving and gracious towards your fellows.

Next, Bill W. says:

> *And let's always remember that **meditation is in reality intensely practical**. One of its first fruits is emotional balance. With it (this new emotional balance through meditation) we can broaden and deepen the channel between ourselves and God as we understand Him.*[64]

> *. . . If you saw your life as a great battle and you **knew** you needed time with God for your very survival, you would do it. Maybe not perfectly—nobody ever does, and that's not the point anyway—but you would have a reason to seek him. We give a half-hearted attempt at the spiritual disciplines when the only reason we have is that we "ought" to. But we'll find a way to make it work when we are convinced we're history if we don't.*[65]

Remember, if it's spiritual, it's practical! Ask yourself the following questions: Am I gaining emotional balance? Is the "*channel*" (the connection between God and me) deepening? These are questions the serious seeker will want to ask. If we

[64] *Ibid.*, p. 101.

[65] John Eldredge, *Wild at Heart*.

are not getting the promised results, we might ask ourselves where we got off track. Go back through the instructions and try it again.[66]

Help From Friends.

This chapter talks about making certain that progress is happening, and how to measure it. I'd like to reiterate that here. In addition to feeling closer to God, hearing God better, and finding His will, His destiny for **you**, try asking your prayer and meditation partners for an honest evaluation from time to time. Remember, "*Iron sharpens iron*!" Or, if you're really brave, ask another close friend, spouse, or relative who is committed to helping you succeed in life. Be sure to ask them to tell you the truth!

NOTES:

____

____

____

____

____

[66] Having said that, this practice will often take some time to "sink down into" and be comfortable with. Like any relationship, my relationship with God strengthens with practice.

Final Thoughts

In 1973, I was addicted to alcohol and drugs. I spent enormous amounts of money each week. I was hopeless, and helpless to stop. I had tried. Then, in one single moment mid-February, a friend of mine led me in a simple prayer, and I was completely free. No desire for substances, no withdrawal, no thoughts of using.

Free.

I still did not understand much about how to keep moving forward in that freedom, and after nearly a decade, slipped backwards into addiction. I did not have the tools I have described to you here. I learned them through trial and failure, and many seasons of difficulty.

Perhaps, like many people trying on sobriety for the first time, or again, your big issue, in your mind, is what to do with this whole notion of God. At least 50% of us in AA's first years faced this dilemma. That percentage probably holds true today as well.

I've included a prayer, similar to the one used by Bill Wilson when he faced this same crossroads in 1934, while a patient once again in Towns Hospital. This prayer, an honest cry from an open heart, has worked for many millions—and I believe it will work for you.

But you must give it a chance—**praying** it, rather than simply **saying** it; then, watch for God to reveal himself to **you**. In your observations, you may want to keep an evidence file of what seem to be God's attempts at making himself known. I think you'll find it interesting; but more than that, I believe you will begin on the road to a new adventure—one I've found worth cherishing now, for over 40 years.

Skeptic's Prayer

God, I don't know whether you even exist. I'm a skeptic. I doubt. I think you may be only a myth. But I'm not certain (at least when I'm completely honest with myself). So if you do exist, and if you really did promise to reward all seekers, you must be hearing me now. So I hereby declare myself a seeker, a seeker of the truth, whatever and wherever it is. I want to know the truth and live the truth. If you are the truth, please help me.

Appendix 1

Some Prayers

St. Francis Prayer

Lord, make me an instrument of your peace;
Where there is hatred, let me sow love;
Where there is injury, your pardon Lord;
Where there's doubt, true faith in you;
O Master,
Grant that I may not so much seek to be consoled as to console;
To be understood, as to understand;
To be loved, as to love;
For it is in giving that we receive,
It is in pardoning that we are pardoned,
And it is in dying that we are born to Eternal Life.
Amen.

(Some versions use "make me a channel"—both are excellent to meditate on.)

Set Aside Prayer

God; please enable me to set aside **everything** I **think** I know, about myself, other people, and especially You, for an open mind, and a new experience, with myself, other people, and especially You.

Appendix 2

STEP 11 – PRAYER EXERCISE

We ask especially for freedom from self-will, and are careful to make no request for ourselves only. We may ask for ourselves if others will be helped.

We are given a guideline in framing our prayers. Is this selfish? Will it also benefit those I am being called to serve ("*God and the people about us*" p. 77). It asks simply that we are not to stop there. ("only"). As an exercise, try to think of something you are praying for that would not help others. I've asked this question to hundreds of people. No one had an answer. So, the question becomes, am I praying for others, too?

Now, make a list of the things you desire for yourself when you pray. Then, ask if others will benefit. Only you can know the answer, because only you can truly know your motives.

Fill out the sheet on the next page; make it your "prayer log" and keep your eyes open for evidence of God answering.

What I Want/Desire/Pray for:	**Will Others Be Helped? (Yes or No)**

Appendix 3

SOME GREAT QUOTES

The greatest gift that can come to anyone is a spiritual awakening. Bill W.

. . .

It takes courage to fulfill your commitments, courage to stay on track, courage to follow your dreams, courage to reach your goals, and courage to walk through your fear. Remember, reaching goals is not so much about doing big things when the feeling hits you; it's more about doing little things every day that move you toward your dream. It's about staying steady and on course. Francine Ward

. . .

The Presence of God

For what we need to know, of course, is not just that God exists, not just that beyond the steely brightness of the stars there is a cosmic intelligence of some kind that keeps the whole show going, but that there is a God right here in the thick of our day-to-day lives who may not be writing messages about himself in the stars but in one way or another is trying to get messages through our blindness as we move around down here knee-deep in the fragrant muck and misery and marvel of the world. It is not objective proof of God's existence that we want, but the experience of God's presence. That is the miracle we are really after, and that is also, I think, the miracle that we really get.

Frank Buechner, *The Magnificent Defeat*

. . .

Wonder

By and large, our world has lost its sense of wonder. We have grown up. We no longer catch our breath at the sight of a rainbow or the scent of a rose, as we once did. We have grown bigger and everything else smaller, less impressive.

Rabbi Abraham Heschel

As civilization advances, the sense of wonder declines. We get so preoccupied with ourselves, the words we speak, the plans and projects we conceive, that we become immune to the glory of creation . . . we grow complacent and lead practical lives. We miss the experience of awe, reverence, and wonder.

Brennan Manning
The Ragamuffin Gospel, pp. 90, 91

. . .

The truth will set you free. But first, it will piss you off. Anonymous

. . .

You can tell the size of your God by looking at the size of your worry list. The longer your list, the smaller your God. Author Unknown

. . .

Maybe the atheist cannot find God for the same reason a thief cannot find a policeman. Author Unknown

BIBLIOGRAPHY

Alcoholics Anonymous, Second Edition (2001). Alcoholics Anonymous World Services, Inc.

Alcoholics Anonymous Comes of Age, a brief history of A.A. (1985). Alcoholics Anonymous Publishing, Inc.

As Bill Sees It (1967). Alcoholics Anonymous World Services, Inc.

Dr. Bob and the Good Oldtimers (1980). Alcoholics Anonymous World Services, Inc.

Lois Remembers, Memoirs of the co-founder of Al-Anon and wife of the co-founder of Alcoholics Anonymous (1979). Anon Family Group Headquarters, Inc.

Robert Thomsen (1975), *Bill W*. Harper & Row.

Twelve Steps and Twelve Traditions (1952). Alcoholics Anonymous World Services, Inc.

Coming Soon!

Many Hearts, One Voice
365 Days of Listening

AND

On Awakening
A Five-CD Set of Meditations, Prayers, and Readings for all Year

www.practicallyspiritualbooks.com